ST. PETER'S
Story

By Marion Thomas • Illustrated By Maria Cristina Lo Cascio

Peter the Fisherman

Luke 5:1-11

Simon Peter fished, by night and by day, on the Sea of Galilee. When he wasn't fishing, Peter mended his nets with his brother, Andrew, and the other fishermen.

One day a man named Jesus came by and told Peter to let down his nets into the water. Peter had been fishing all night—and hadn't caught one fish. But he did as Jesus asked. Then the net became so filled with fish that Peter needed help dragging it to shore!

Peter fell at Jesus' feet, amazed and humbled.

"Don't be afraid," Jesus told him. "Follow me, and you will catch more than these fish. You will be catching people."

Peter with Jesus the Healer

Luke 5:17-26; 8:49-56; Mark 7:31-37; 10:46-52

Peter followed Jesus, by night and by day, with his brother, Andrew, his friends, James and John, and eight other men. These twelve men were Jesus' apostles. They had all been chosen by Jesus to be his special friends.

Peter saw Jesus heal many people. A man who was blind could now see! A man who was deaf could now hear! A man who was disabled could walk again! Peter even saw Jesus bring a little girl back to life. The little girl's parents were so happy that their daughter was alive again.

Peter with Jesus the Teacher

Matthew 6:19-21, 25-33

Peter listened to Jesus, by night and by day, as he taught the people about their heavenly Father's great love for them.

"Don't worry," Jesus told them. "Look at the birds. My Father won't let them go hungry. Look at the wild flowers in the fields. God makes them beautiful. God loves you even more than these flowers and birds. Make God the most important person in your life, and he will take great care of you.

"Be good to people who need your help. Store up treasure for yourself in heaven, where no moths can destroy it and no thieves can steal it away."

Peter with Jesus the Messiah

Matthew 8:23-27; 14:15-21, 25-32; 16:13-16

Peter watched Jesus, by night and by day, and realized that he was no ordinary man.

Peter saw Jesus calm a storm while his friends clung to the boat in fear. He saw Jesus take five pieces of bread and two little fish and provide enough food for thousands of people—with twelve baskets left over. He saw Jesus walk on water—and Peter did the same thing, but when his faith began to fail and he started to sink, Jesus caught him.

"Who do you think I am?" Jesus asked his disciples one day.

"You are the Messiah, the Son of the living God," Peter replied.

"You are Peter, the rock, and upon this rock I will build my Church," Jesus told him.

Peter at the Last Supper

Luke 22:7-23; John 13:1-9, 31-38

Peter walked with Jesus, by night and by day, until they came into Jerusalem to celebrate the Passover feast.

He went with John to the upstairs room where they ate their Last Supper together. He let Jesus wash his feet—the task of a servant. He shared in the bread that Jesus said was his body, broken for them. He drank from the cup of wine that Jesus said was his blood, shed for them.

"I won't betray you," Peter told Jesus. "I would rather die for you!"

"Peter, Peter," Jesus answered, "before the cock crows, you will deny three times that you even know me."

Peter in Gethsemane

Matthew 26:36-56, Luke 22:39-53

Peter promised to keep watch, by night, as Jesus prayed in the
Garden of Gethsemane. Instead of staying awake with Jesus,
however, Peter fell asleep. Jesus knew that he was going to die
a terrible death, but he said to his heavenly Father, "Not as I
want, but as you want." Then Jesus woke up Peter and the other
disciples.

When soldiers came with torches and swords to arrest
Jesus, Peter cut off the right ear of the high priest's slave—and
watched as Jesus healed him. The other disciples fled, and Peter
stood by helplessly as Jesus was taken away.

Peter Denies Jesus

Matthew 26:69-75; Luke 22:54-62

Peter waited, by night, as Jesus was questioned by the high priest. He kept to the shadows, avoiding the glances of the people in the courtyard.

"This is one of his friends," a servant girl said, pointing to Peter.

"No, I don't know him," replied Peter.

"Surely this man was with Jesus," said another servant girl.

"No, not me," said Peter angrily.

"Listen to his accent—he even comes from Galilee!" someone else added.

"I don't know what you are talking about!" Peter said.

Then the cock crowed, and Jesus turned around to look at Peter. When Peter saw him, he remembered what Jesus had said and went away weeping.

17

Peter at the Empty Tomb

John 20:1-10, 19-23

Peter stayed away, by night and by day, as Jesus was condemned to death. He could not watch as Jesus was mocked, whipped, and crucified. Peter knew that Jesus had been buried in a nearby tomb on Friday, just before sundown. He was very sad and very afraid.

But on Sunday morning, when Mary Magdalene came running to tell the disciples that the tomb was empty, Peter ran with John to see what had happened.

Peter saw the empty tomb and the linen cloths lying folded because Jesus was no longer there.

When Peter returned to the other disciples, Jesus came into the locked room where they were staying and said to them, "Peace be with you." Jesus was very much alive!

19

Peter and the Risen Lord

John 21:1-19

Peter went fishing, by night, in the Sea of Galilee with some of his friends.

When the sun rose over the hills, Peter's nets were still empty. Then he heard the voice of a man calling him from the shore, telling him to throw the net over the other side once more. Peter did so, and as the nets filled up with so many fish, he knew that this man was Jesus!

"Do you love me, Peter?" Jesus asked over breakfast.

"Yes, Lord, you know that I love you," Peter replied.

Jesus asked Peter the same question two more times. And Peter answered in the same way each time.

Then Jesus said, "I have work for you to do. Feed my sheep. Look out for all of my friends, and tell everyone about me."

Peter at Pentecost

Acts 1:12-14; 2:1-40

Peter prayed with the disciples, by night and by day.

Jesus had promised to send the Holy Spirit to them. So in an

upstairs room, together with Jesus' mother and the disciples, Peter

waited and prayed. On the day of Pentecost, they heard the sound of

a mighty wind filling the house and saw a column of fire coming down

and separating onto each one of them. Peter knew that Jesus had kept

his promise. Now they were no longer afraid. The Holy Spirit had

given them the courage to preach the good news.

"You saw that Jesus was sent by God. You saw that he performed

miracles," Peter said to the crowd. "Yet you let him die alone on a

cross. We are here to tell you that God raised him from death—and we

have seen him! He is ready to forgive anyone who comes to him."

Peter the Healer

Acts 2:41-47; 3:1-8; 9:32-42

Peter rejoiced, by day and by night, because thousands of people believed in Jesus and received forgiveness for their sins. Peter saw the new believers sharing everything they had with each other and with people in need. Peter saw healing miracles performed in Jesus' name.

"Please help me," a man outside the temple asked him. "Have you some money to give a man who cannot walk?"

"I have no money to give you," Peter replied, "but I have an even greater gift. In the name of Jesus, stand up and walk!"

Peter also healed a man named Aeneas and a woman named Tabitha. He traveled from place to place, sharing the good news of Jesus with everyone he met.

Peter's Vision

Acts 10:1-48

Peter followed the Holy Spirit, by day and by night, doing whatever the Spirit told him. One day Peter had a vision that puzzled him. Just then, men sent by a Roman soldier named Cornelius appeared and invited Peter to come to his house. A Jewish person could not enter the house of a person who was not Jewish. But Peter knew from the vision that God wanted him to go.

So Peter went to the Cornelius' home and told everyone there about Jesus. When God blessed them with the gift of the Holy Spirit, Peter baptized them. Peter now knew that the message of God's love and forgiveness was for everyone, not just for the Jewish people.

Peter's Suffering

Acts 12:1-19

Peter suffered in prison, by day and by night, because King Herod was angry that he was spreading the good news about Jesus. Peter waited, bound in chains between soldiers, while his friends prayed to God for his safety and deliverance.

One night Peter watched in amazement as an angel removed his chains and led him safely past all the guards and out of the prison to freedom.

Peter knew that God had plans for him, plans to lead his Church as the first pope. He was to love and serve the people in his care, just as Jesus had loved him. Peter was so filled with the power of the Holy Spirit that he was no longer afraid, and he willingly gave his life for Jesus and his Church. Today he is in heaven with all the saints. Ask St. Peter to pray for you, especially when you need courage and boldness to share about Jesus!

First edition 2012

Published in the U.S. and Canada by
The Word Among Us Press
7115 Guilford Drive,
Frederick, Maryland 21704

www.wau.org

ISBN: 978-1-59325-196-3

Publishing Director: Annette Reynolds
Art Director: Gerald Rogers
Pre-production Manager: Krystyna Kowalska Hewitt
Production Manager: John Laister

Printed and bound in Singapore
October 2012